George Grenville

A Letter to the Right Honourable George Grenville, esq.

Upon the conduct of the late opposition

George Grenville

A Letter to the Right Honourable George Grenville, esq.
Upon the conduct of the late opposition

ISBN/EAN: 9783337195793

Printed in Europe, USA, Canada, Australia, Japan

Cover: Foto ©Suzi / pixelio.de

More available books at **www.hansebooks.com**

A

LETTER

To the Right Honourable

George Grenville, Efq;

&c. &c. &c.

Upon the CONDUCT of the

LATE Oppofition.

LONDON:

Printed for W. NICOLL, in *St. Paul's Church-Yard.* 1764.

A

LETTER,

&c.

S I R,

YOUR Opening of the State of the Nation, towards the Clofe of the laſt Seſſion, diſplayed a Knowledge, accurate and extenſive, of the Subject which you treated, in the Opinion of every Man who heard you. The Enemies of your Power, by rendering reluctant Juſtice to your Abilities, have given a ſingular Proof of the Force of Truth, con-

B ſtantly

ftantly refufed to the ableft of your Predeceffors by the Oppofers of their Days.

Th· Effects of this Perfuafion have
· ·d appear in all who are
·ly · poffeffed with other
which warp even the upright
the Interefts of Ambition, Want,
·nment. Nor is the Power of Con-
· totally loft even upon thefe; and
· it operates more fenfibly upon o-
Defpondency of Succefs damps the
·r of a Purfuit, which the Hope of
·ding infpired.

· have explained our Condition to us;
f there was a Man before uncon-
·, that the late glorious and fuccef-
·r would have been fatal in its fur-
· Progrefs, you have convinced him of
· Error; and the moft enthufiaftic Wor-
· ppers of that great Minifter, who in-
· red and directed our military Opera-
·ns, do not wifh his Return into Power,
for

for a further Diſplay of his Abilities in conquering.

Incomparable as theſe are in that Scene, they might fail him and us in another claiming equal Talents; but as widely different as Expence and Frugality, Debts and Savings, the Sword that makes the Wound and the Salve that heals it, War and Peace. The Genius, the Temper, and Diſpoſition of Mind, which are beſt adapted to the Direction of theſe Contraries, and the Arts by which they ſhould be directed, are equally contrariant; too oppoſite to exiſt in the ſame Man: while the Knowledge earned by Experience in one of theſe Situations, becomes an uſeleſs Acquiſition in the other.

Quickneſs of Perception, Capacity of Thought, Preciſion of Judgment, and Elevation of Sentiment, are the Gifts of Nature, which, with little Experience, have in a few Inſtances produced Prodigies in the Field; and, in our great War-Miniſter,

have

have produced a Prodigy in the Cabinet: But, neceffary as thefe Qualities are in your Station, they never can do alone, and unaffifted by long and diligent Service; a heaven-born Financer never dropt from the Sky compleatly fitted for Bufinefs: He muft deal in Details, to be Mafter of that Whole, which refults from them. The Bufinefs of every Office is his, and com-pofes but one Part of his Studies: He muft know the State of thofe Things from which Revenue arifes, of Produce, Ma-nufacture, and Commerce, throughout the wide Extent of home and foreign Mar-kets, in the various Viciffitudes of each; for on thefe that great Syftem of Taxa-tion depends, under which Nations flourifh or are undone.

Of thefe our late Minifter confeffes him-felf ignorant; nor would he in any one Inftance, during his fole Direction of other Affairs, interfere in thefe. He left that Province entire to the noble Perfon who prefided at the Board of Treafury; and

were

were he to return into Power, that high Office, incomparably the moſt important in times of Peace, muſt be entruſted in other Hands. What thoſe might be, and for whom that Truſt was deſigned in the laſt Autumn's Conference, much and variouſly talked off, I ſhall not preſume to gueſs : but thus far I may ſay, the noble Duke, and the honourable Gentleman who had been twice ſucceſſively Chancellor of the Exchequer under his Adminiſtration, were not reported to have been the Objects of our great Commoner's Deſignation, or if they had, with all the Juſtice due to the Characters of both, and without entering into any inviduous Compariſon of Talents, the advanced Age of the one, not a Member of the Houſe of Commons, and the declining State of Health in the other, who never appeared there as firſt in the miniſterial Line, and was but ſecond at his own Board, leave that Preference with you, which belongs to an applauded Arrangement of our Finances without Doors, and to an able Support of your own Admini-ſtration

ftration within. Whatever the Pretences
of others may be, as they have not been
tried in this Sphere, they remain fubject to
an Uncertainty, too hazardous for Experiment, in a Station upon which the Salvation
of our Country depends.

The prefent Conteft therefore, between
Mr. *Pitt* and you, is not in that Scene
where he has demonftrated unrivaled Abilities ; for, Fraife be to God, War no
longer rages : and the Queftion, reduced
to its proper State, refts upon this fingle
Point ; whether, in a total Change of Situation, his acknowledged Merit in what is
paft and over, gives him a Preference ad-
vantageous to his Country in its prefent
State : a Meafure as irrational and dangerous, as its Contrary would have been, had
the Seals and the Helm been forcibly
fnatched from his Hands to confide them
in yours, at a Time when the fole Guidance
of War required an Experience, which you
had not ; and Talents peculiarly adapted

to that Crifis, of which you had given no Proofs.

Such Preferences can only be wifhed for by a Spirit of Partiality, often fpringing from Principles that no Party will avow, and which the Pride of Man fometimes conceals even from the Bofom they infpire. But the Fallacy is eafily detected by the impartial Obferver ; and if one be prefered to an other, for inconclufive Reafons, or, which is ftill ftronger, Reafons that conclude againft him, unprejudiced Men will not be at a Lofs to affign the real Caufe : And, whatever the Pretences to Patriotifm may be, fuch illogical Reafoning marks with the indelible Character of Faction, that Party where it obvioufly prevails.

Minifters may owe their Support to the fame Motives upon which an Oppofition to them may be founded : and their Fitnefs or Unfitnefs for the Pofts they fill, is the only Criterion, by which the contending Sides can or ought to be tryed. This Teft

is

·s infallible ; but the Difficulty *lies* in applying it fairly, where all are interested, and every Man measures the same Object with a Standard of his own.

Innumerable are the Paffions, which form the various Tempers and Complexions of Men, too many and too oppofite to exift at the same Inftant in the same Breaft : Liberality excludes Sordidnefs, Pity melts Hatred away, and Love extinguifhes Refentment ; but any one of thefe, and of many more, is often too ftrong for Reafon and Juftice to contend with. In a Multitude they all conftantly exift, and may frequently be found cooperating and affifting in the same Direction, towards the same Purpofes : the Avarice of one may be fupplyed by the overflowing Generofity of another, fneaking Craft foar on the Wings of Spirit, and climbing Ambition mount the long-practifed Ladder of humble and undefigning Honefty.

Thefe

There never was a Time, when a greater Variety of Caufes concurred in exciting all the different Emotions of which the human Heart is fufceptible; and in binding together the various Tempers and Difpofitions of Men, thro' all Conditions, Ranks, and Ages; nor ever were more Art and Induftry employed in producing and preferving this Union, by two Sets of wily Veterans, adverfe when in Power, but tho' never joined by Love now agreeing in one common Hatred, the ftrongeft and moft lafting Cement in political Difgrace. The Friends of thefe pointed to a popular Minifter in the Meridian of his Glory funk into Retirement, foon followed by an old Servant of the Crown, illuftrious from his Family, Titles and Fortune, and ftill more recommended by that Fortune impaired in Offices, which were wont to enrich others, and by a Refufal of every pecuniary Affiftance offered by his Sovereign at his Departure from his Prefence.

Another Great Nobleman offered himself to view, equally diftinguifhed by Family, Title and Eftate, amiable in his Manners, and refpectable for his Virtues, difmiffed from the higheft Poft about the Perfon of the Crown, and erafed from the numerous Lift of his Counfellors in a Strain of unufual Severity. Thefe were voluntarily accompanyed by many others, fome their Equals or near their Equals in Rank, connected in Principle, Friendfhip and Blood, divefted like them of thofe Enfigns of Favour, which long Prefcription had taught themfelves and others to confider as hereditary Rights ; while a numerous Train of Dependants, driven from Plenty and Comfort into Penury and Want, compofed the Rear of this interefting Spectacle.

Here were Objects formed to affect every Temper, and to infpire every Paffion, fuited to every State and Condition of the Spectators, bringing what they faw home to their own Bofoms, and interefting Self-love

in

in the Fate of others: and there were Spectators of every State and Condition, who, thus operated upon, joined the Sufferers, adopting their Cause and their Resentments. Admiration, Respect and Pity are kindred Senfations, and blended together beget Indignation, Hatred, and Revenge against the Enemies of their favoured Objects. Nor were there other Circumftances wanting to heighten the Scene.

Of those who succeeded to Power the Chief stood high in the Personal Favour of his Sovereign, which could only be equaled by the Envy and Malice of those, whose Pride suffered under a marked Preference, by them stiled Disgrace. Diffatisfaction was not confined to thefe; the Inftances which Hiftory affords of an Abufe of personal Influence over the Minds of our Princes, render the Name of Favourite traditionally ungracious to the Multitude, who are taught from what they have heard or read, to annex indifcriminately, and often unjuftly, to that Word the Ideas of a

Spencer

Spencer or a *Gaveston.* And he who suddenly aspires to a dangerous Preeminence over his Fellow-Subjects, without Time or Opportunities to form Connections, and bind by Benefits the Affections of Men to him tryed and experienced in a gradual Progress to Power, is destitute of such Advocates to plead for and support his Elevation, while the Velocity of his Rise makes the Object more striking, than if mounting by flower Degrees, the Eyes of Men had been insensibly accustomed to see him rise. Obnoxious from these Circumstances the late Minister was born a *Scotchman*, in him an original Sin, not to be expiated by many Virtues, and a Blemish on his Birth not to be cleared by hereditary Titles, nor by his Alliance with some of the best Blood of *England*, which ensured, to a Branch of his Family, Possessions on this side of the *Tweed*, equal to those which enrich the Stems of our most opulent Nobility. But his Preferment offended the Plebian as much as the Patrician : National Pride was hurt ; a *Scot* at the Head of the Treasury

was

was not to be endured by an *English* Porter, fweating beneath his Burthen ; and the Cobler reecho'd from his Stall, to his Brethren in Common-Council affembled, No Favourite, no Statefman. Almoft every Corporation in *England* caught the Alarm, bleating after thofe Bell-weathers of Faction, who in the Heart of the Metropolis dared to infult their Royal Gueft, by a Treatment injurious, even to the Rights of Hofpitality.

The moft abandoned Wretch that ever difgraced private Life, with Talents only known by an Abufe of them, rofe from the Obfcurity of mean Birth, and a fcanty Fortune earned by domeftic Villainy, and confumed in low Debauchery, the Champion of Virtue, Liberty, and *England*. A virtuous, but unpopular Minifter, foon proved an unequal Match for fuch an Affailant. But the Triumph of Vice did not end here : He became a Rival even to him in whofe Vindication he firft drew his Pen ; and the loved, the admired, Commoner funk fecond

in

in Popularity to thofe ruffian Talents, which
defended and difgraced his Caufe. I have
ftated thefe Facts in an Inftance not to be
parallelled, as the ftrongeft Proofs of the
Temper of the Nation, prepared to re-
ceive very unfavourable Impreffion from the
moft unworthy Hands. If the Colourings
of this Picture be thought too glaring and
over-charged, let thofe anfwer for me
who encouraged, vindicated and applauded
the Man, whom they after deferted and
reviled, when the Arm of Parliamentary
Juftice was ftretched out againft him, and
he fell an unaffifted and unpitied Victim to
that abufed Authority, the moft facred in
civil Society, which he dared to contemn
and violate.

The Tories, long accuftomed to be treated
as Jacobites by the minifterial Party, whom
they were wont invariably to oppofe, and
who had received the like Treatment from
their former oppofing Friends after they had
rifen upon them into Power, had, forget-
ting recent Injuries, ranged themfelves under

der the Banners of a Minister, reconciled to
them by their loved Epithet of *Patriot*, in
Contradistinction to others. In the Opening of a new Reign, under a gracious De-
claration from the Throne, they received
an Earnest in some Instances of that Pro-
scription being removed, which had since
the Accession of this Royal Family branded
and distinguished them from the prevailing
Party. Some were placed in honourable
Stations, suited to their Rank, near the Per-
son of their Sovereign; and if none were
intrusted with Departments of Business and
Influence, a Consciousness of Inability, from
want of Experience, accounted to their own
Minds for this Exclusion. They felt the
whole of their Obligation; and acknowledged a Part of it as derived from him who
was the avowed Channel of Favour, with
whom they remained, a few excepted,
firmly connected in the Separation which
soon after ensued.

The Charge of Jacobitism was now revived by the discontented and seceeding
Whigs,

Whigs, and by a ftrange Inverfion of Argument, they who were formerly condemned as diffaffected, becaufe they oppofed, were now marked with the fame
opprobrious Character becaufe they affifted
Government; while their few recufant Brethren of the Cocoa Tree were the only
loyal Subjects, who bore the Name of Tory.
Thefe concurred with difcontented Whigs
in lamenting a Change of Syftem, by
which old and faithful Servants were difmiffed to make room for a new Tribe: nor
is this the only Inftance of Ideas of hereditary Right transferred from the Crown to
certain Families, which, fince the Acceffion of this Royal Family, have from Father
to Son exercifed all its Functions, and confidered their Mafters, like the Scepter which
they bore, as mere Emblems of Regality,
which virtually and in its Effects refided in
them.

The Times were however fitted for fuch
Doctrine: Licentioufnefs in talking, writ-
ing and acting were Liberty; while **the**

beft

beft known, the moft neceffary, and
therefore the oftneft practifed, Powers
of Prerogative, in placing or difplacing
the Servants of the Crown, were arbitrary,
Infringements of that independant Freedom
which this Family was chofen to defend ;
and in thofe Preludes to ftill more dangerous Defigns, concurring Tories were, by
their Principles, the fitteft and moft ready
Inftruments. Such was the general Lan-
guage : and while thefe Fears and thefe
Jealoufies, affected by the Artful, and really
exifting in the Weak, revived and kindled
the expiring Embers of Party, induftrioufly
fupplyed with every combuftible Matter,
an ill-timed, and at all times an ill concerted
Tax upon Cyder was haftily introduced
towards the Clofe of the Seffion of Parliament, which almoft folely affecting five
Tory Counties, difobliged many of their
Reprefentatives, and totally eftranged fome
from the Support of a Minifter, who, loaded
with an Odium partly contracted on their
Account, felt his Burthen encreafe by the
additional Weight of their Refentment.

The

The evil Confequences of this Meafure, lafted longer than the Power of its Author, and the fucceeding Adminiftration experienced its Effects, even after the Tax had been reduced to a very moderate Compofition, and the Rigour of the Mode of Collection relaxed by every Indulgence that you could devife.

When the firft Bill for impofing this Tax had paffed thro' both Houfes of Parliament, the Corporation of the City of London, who infolently call themfelves the City, and ufurping the Name, would affume an Importance not belonging even to that great Metropolis, feized fo fair an Opportunity of controlling every Branch of the Legiflature ; and petitioned the King to withhold his Royal Affent, by an Exercife of Prerogative never ufed fince thefe Nations have been bleffed with this *Brunfwick* Line, and but once fince the Revolution redeemed us from thofe Tyrants, who were fond of fubftituting Will in Place of Law. The Petitioners went ftill farther, and with an Ignorance

norance and Inconfiftency natural to mean
Men, who afpire beyond their Sphere, ad-
vifed our Monarch, from a tender Concern
for Liberty, to venture upon what never
was attempted even by the *Stuart* Race;
and, by rejecting one part of the Bill only,
for fuch was the Prayer of their Petition,
give the Force of Law to a mutilated Act of
the Legiflature, modelled- and abridged by
the fole Pleafure of the Crown.

But whatever our Surprife might then
have been, we fhould now ceafe to wonder at this Inftance of abfurd Inconfiftency
in a few ignorant Tradefmen, when we
have lately feen a Propofition for interpo-
fing a Refolution of the Houfe of Commons
between Law and a judicial Determination, the Caufe actually depending in thofe
Courts, where alone it is conftitutionally
cognifable; and to encreafe the Wonder,
that Propofition was in a full Houfe of Parliament rejected only by a Majority of fourteen Voices; 232 to 218: for fuch was
the Queftion, upon the Succefs of which

the

the *Monument* of *London* was to have blazed as a Signal of Deliverance from a more threatning Conflagration than that which this Fabrick was erected to commemorate*.

Who the real Incendiaries were can surely not be a Doubt; thofe Secretaries by whofe Warrant Mr. *Wilkes* and his Papers had been feized, drawn in the ufual Form which had prevailed from the Revolution down to its Date, often produced during that Period in the Courts of Juftice, and never once objected to ; or thofe who inflamed the Nation with all the Virulence, Falfhood, and Abufe, as if the Liberty of the Subject had been invaded by a new and arbitrary Stretch of Authority. Yet when the Bufinefs was brought to a fair Iffue, thofe very Men and their Friends and Affociates difclaimed all Perfonal Accufation ;

---

* The *Monument* was to have been illuminated, and Beer to be given to the Populace, to gladden the Hearts of the enlightened Freemen of *London*.

the

the Hands that figned the Warrants, the Capital Offenders, if there had been Offence, were not even named in the Queftion ; nor could they have been named, without involving in any Cenfure to be paffed upon them, thofe Chiefs of the Oppofition, who had before held the fame Seals; one of whom, as he had been longeft in Office, was incomparably the moft frequent Tranfgreffor ; and the other, formed to exceed in whatever he undertakes, paffed thofe Bounds obferved by the leaft cautious of his Predeceffors. One peculiar Circumftance rendered Inaccuracy the lefs excufable in him, who had, or might have had, the Affiftance of that great Magiftrate, then the firft Law-Servant of the Crown, who in the Seat of Judgment had difcovered an Informality, which efcaped the Vigilance of all who went before him, foon after he had, in the Capacity of Attorney General, profecuted to Conviction and Punifhment an infamous Offender, whofe Papers as well as Perfon had been feized for publifhing a falfe and feditious Libel.

But

But in truth the Practice, however excusable from long and uniform Usage, was not warranted by Law; this was equally the Doctrine of both Sides, and that Doctrine was sure of being confirmed by the unanimous Opinion of *Westminster-hall*, in the necessary Course of a Proceeding, which had already obtained the Determination of one Court in its Favour.

The Merit of Condemning this Practice, as far as any had Merit, was common to all; but the Guilt of stirring up the Nation by unfounded Falshoods, was entirely theirs, who at first devised them as an Engine to excite Compassion towards the Martyr in their Cause, the favorite Reviler of Majesty and Parliamentary Authority. But when the Weight of his Crimes bore him down, and would have dragged them with him, had they adhered to their Promises of inseparable Connection and Support, they tried the Force of a popular Topic upon honest but unwary Minds.

They

They meant to deceive and divide the Friends of Adminiftration. They meant to obtain that Superiority by thofe Means, which they had vainly attempted by all others, and a Victory *now*, they confidered as a compleat Conqueft. For this Purpofe a Queftion was devifed, to which as a fimple Propofition, no Man could refufe his Affent ; and the Parliamentary Expedient of putting off a Queftion upon which it would not be proper for either Houfe fingly to decide, had been too often ufed for other Purpofes, where that Impropriety did not exift, to fatisfy Men warm in an Inftance which feemed to decide whether their own Perfons, Papers and Houfes were fafe from Meffengers, wantonly and implicitly executing the Orders of their Superiors. The fhorteft Sufpence feemed too long, during which an Uncertainty remained, whether we were at that Inftant Freemen or Slaves. Arguments, which in this Inftance did not conclude, for the Provifion offered was inadequate to the Evil, had

any

any new Provision been neceffary ; and
which in their utmost Latitude would conclude againft the Checks provided by the
Wifdom of our mixed Conftitution, to
fecure the Acts of Legiflature from Surprife,
Paffion, Ignorance, and Error. However,
thefe Arguments were urged with all that
Force of Self-Conviction, which feducive
Eloquence affumes unconvinced ; and it
had its Effect upon fome, who by their Example offered a Sanction to others, cool
Friends or difguifed Enemies to Adminiftration. Befide, the Apprehenfions of
Impreffions made upon their Conftituents
by a firft Glance, which could only be effa-
ced by a Debate they did not hear, and by
Deductions of Reafon, which require more
Knowledge and Attention than the Multitude is able or willing to beftow, hung over
the Minds of many, and compofed that
motley Divifion, in which a confiderable
Number of Placemen, and near half the
Tories, concurred with oppofing Whigs.

But

But the Fate of another Propofition,
which foon was offered for doing that conftitutionally and effectually by a more com-
prehenfive Law, difcovered to all, who
would fee, the Motives that actuated the
Leaders of Oppofition. That Motion was
thinly attended by their Party, and ftrenu-
oufly oppofed by thofe who did attend ; juft
as the Refolution would have been had it come
from Friends to the Adminiftration ; for it is
impoffible to fuppofe they would have pre-
ferred improper and ineffectual Means to
the more proper and adequate, if the Service of their Country made any confiderable Part of their Object. To carry a Queftion againft the Minifter was their View,
and when that failed, they laid afide, for
the Ufe of fome future Day, the Pageantry
of painted Terrors, with which, like po-
pifh Priefts, they would awe thofe they
mean to govern ; and the watchful Patriots,
who could not fleep under Apprehenfion of
ruffian Meffengers breaking in upon them,
have fince enjoyed their peaceful Slumbers

E   uninterrupted

uninterrupted by the Clank of vifionary Chains.

When the Earl of *Bute* had quitted that high Poft to which you fucceeded, he undoubtedly had a fuperior Claim to the Merit of thofe Meafures, with all who approved them, of which he was confidered as the fole Author by others, and as fuch fingled out the deftined Victim of National Vengeance, for a ruinous and ignominious Peace. Your Share of Power at that Period neither entitled you to any large Proportion of Praife from one Side, nor rendered you an Object of Hatred to the other : You never was fuppofed to influence the Councils of that firft Minifter ; and you was known to be little fhort of an avowed Enemy to Mr. *Fox*; who, in Preference to you, was entrufted by him to take the Lead in the Houfe of Commons : You was free from all the Objections perfonal to either, and ftood only refponfible for what had been done fince your Acceffion to Power. You neither turned thofe out who had been difplaced,

placed, nor filled their Pofts with thofe who fucceeded to them. As, therefore, you had little or no Share in the Caufes of Difcontent, you ought to have been fafe from the Refentment of Injuries, and fo you would have been, had Meafures been the Object of Oppofition, or Men under any other Defcription but that which would exclude all alike, who dared to hold what the Junto had an indefeafible Right to enjoy. Had you been what Lord *Bute* was, and you now are, or had he been born like you in the Vale of *Aylefbury*, the Oppofition would have been the fame ; and fome other Objections found equally ftrong, as thofe drawn from the Place of his Nativity. Could any Doubt remain upon the Truth of this Suppofition, the higheft Attention to the Conduct of his and now your Enemies, puts it beyond Controverfy.

When he firft refigned, they fuppofed or would have others fuppofe, that his Influence remained in its full Force, manifefted in all that was done while the di-

recting

recting Agent remained concealed. With
what Truth this was urged, and, if at all true,
in what degree, I shall not venture to de-
termine. But however that may have been,
when his Retirement into the Country and
the Prudence of his Conduct there, had
given unequivocal Proofs of at least an al-
tered Purpose; when the present Admini-
stration evidently stood upon a Self-suppor-
ted Basis, then Opposition changed its Lan-
guage : The once arbitrary Minister was
said to be driven into Exile by his more des-
potic and unrelenting Successors, and the
Sweets of private Friendship denied to a
great King by the Insolence of an imperi-
ous Divan, presuming to give Law to their
Sovereign, in the most insolent Manner.
Even in the Privacies of his Friendship, they
have made their Benefactor eat his Bread
in Lanishment, and this under the specious
Colour of delivering Majesty from a pre-
tended Intention of the same kind of Ty-
ranny in others. Such are the bitter La-
mentations, and such the tender Feelings
for our amiable Monarch and his constant
Friend,

Friend, in a Letter addreſſed by one of the dutiful, modeſt, conſiſtent, *Cotterie* in *Albemarle-ſtreet*, to the *Cocoa-tree* in *Pallmall*.

Nay, if Fame ſpeaks Truth, and the Report has not been contradicted, the once deteſted and deteſtable *Scot*, who was to have been dragged from behind the Throne to exemplary and condign Puniſhment, has been very lately courted to exert that Influence, which he was ſuppoſed to have concealed for the ſurer Deſtruction of *England*, and to return into Power, glorious and exalted, in friendly Union with the Patriot-Miniſter, upon the Shoulders of *Engliſh* Patriots. Such was the firſt Meaſure inſpired by Hope, dawning upon Oppoſition thro' a ſlender Majority of fourteen, and ſuch the Means deviſed to render Succeſs infallible. But the extraordinary Ambaſſador, deputed to the baniſhed Stateſman for this Purpoſe, had the Misfortune to ſtumble at his Threſhold, ominous Preſage! and was refuſed an Audience.

Imme-

Immediately previous to that noble Lord's Retirement, it is very true that the Hero of Oppofition, by whom, and many others, *Englifh* Liberty is faid to fwear, in the Letter from *Albemarle-ftreet*, as the *Greeks* did, *per cæfos in Marathone, et Salamine, Propugnatores Reipublicæ*, far from wifhing him exiled, had a private Meeting with him; and in a fubfequent Conferrence with a greater Perfonage, is fuppofed not to have been unfriendly to him in the Terms dictated to his R——l Mafter; Terms, whatever they were, fpurned by indignant Majefty; and fuch as the now befriended Earl, in Duty and Affection to his Sovereign, thought lefs eligible than a voluntary Banifhment from his Prefence.

Thefe are Facts, which afford fo broad a Cement upon what is lefs precifely known of that dark Tranfaction, that it requires fomething more to confute it than a fupercilious Silence, fcorning to give itfelf even the Trouble of contradicting a prepofterous

Heap

Heap of abfurd Falfhoods. Vide Letter from *Albemarle-ftreet.*

There are Actions eafier to be denied than juftified ; and a contemptuous Silence requires lefs Hardinefs of Front than an audacious Enterprize. There are Difpofitions which prompt to both. But is it then falfe; that the Perfon confidently employed in the firft Steps of this Negotiation, was the loweft Tool of a late Minifter, himfelf held unworthy by our great Commoner, of any Participation of Power under his Adminiftration? Is it not true that this bafe Inftrument had rendered himfelf ftill more infamous, by a recent Treachery againft that Mafter, who raifed him from native Beggary to incredible Opulence ! and if all this be true, can any thing be fuppofed more prepofterous than the Choice of fuch a Vehicle, to convey the pure Breathings of Patriotic Spirit to the Ears of Royalty, mifguided and deluded by bad Men ? Is there after this, any thing prepofterous that may not be credited of the fame Man ?

Is

Is the Suppofition abfurd, that he fhould liften to a Reconciliation to the Earl of *Bute*, who reviled Sir *Robert Walpole* living, and after his Death courted the Favour of his Friends by offering Incenfe to his Memory; who defpifed Mr. *Pelham*, and ferved under him ; who in Turns extolled and depreffed his Brother by Flattery and Abufe, as either ferved his Purpofe ; who, when in Oppofition, treated thofe Minifters he oppofed as Betrayers of their Country ; and when their Affociate in Adminiftration, as Fools unable to ferve it, fnatching the whole Guidance from their Hands, and borrowing (in his own Phrafe) their Majority, to vote as he directed, mixed with honeft, independant Country-Gentlemen, who, once indeed (to ufe again his own Words) paved the Streets of *Oxford* with Jacobites. Yet thofe very Minifters are the Chiefs whofe Fall he now laments, buried in the Ruins of their Country ; while as many of that Majority as adhere to them, are now cannonized as heroick Sufferers, Victims to inanimate Tory-Idols,

Idols, once more converted by the Charms of his Magic, into their primitive Sub-ftance.

Or is it abfurd to believe (what by the bye Nineteen in Twenty do believe) that he, who took Advantage of the Confufion of his Country, to force himfelf upon his King, in the late Reign, fhould repeat the Experiment in this, and avail himfelf of infatuated Prejudices and public Clamour, to prefcribe Terms to our Sovereign, which would have been injurious to the Honour of a private Man. But a Difavowal of Meafures, folemnly approved, and Ter-giverfation from Opinions, publickly de-clared, are Meafures of patriot Oppofition, which, fanctified by the frequent Example of its Chief, became a Model, worthy to be prefented to the Lord of Nations, for his Adoption.

Thefe Suppofitions compofe that Heap, of which the Letter-writer complains; and to prove them falfe, furpaffes the Skill of a

F   futile,

futile, obfcure, analitic Sophifter ; who. from the Lees of Falfhood would be thought to extract the Spirit of Truth, with. fomething which ftirs the fermenting Quality of Liberty. *P. 5.* and whofe heatlefs Laboratory has little of Fire, except the Smoke that furrounds it. If this Pedlar in harmlefs Poifons, cannot plead the Excufe of Poverty, he as far exceeds *Romeo*'s Apothecary in Guilt, as he falls fhort of him in Arts of Mifchief. *P. 33.*

Such is that Writer, the Champion of the *Cotterie,* who in the moft perplexed, inconfiftent, and unintelligible Rhapfody of falfe Metaphor, unmeaning Subtlety, and embaraffed Stile, dares to lay a *heavy* Charge, at leaft in one Senfe of the Word, upon the fulleft, the cleareft and moft irrefragable Argument, that could engage the Attention of an admiring Audience ; treated by him, as a long laborious and fallacious Declamation. But Abufe is the only Praife fuch a Hand can beftow, which an honeft Man would not be afhamed of receiving. You, Sir,

Sir, have an ample Share of it; and it is
juſt you ſhould in a Performance, which
ſtigmatiſes all who worthily ſerve the
Crown, and cooperate with them in the Service of their Country, as rotten Tories
combined with rotten Whigs: Men of
flagitious Characters, looſe Principles, abandoned in their Morals, deſperate in Fortune, &c. &c. &c. without one ſingle Ex-
ception; ſuch are the wretched Gleanings
of *Wilkes*'s and *Churchill*'s Harveſt.

The Fable of *Proteus*, often applied to
Duplicity and Deceit, ſeems peculiarly em-
blematical of Faction; by turns wild and
untameable as the brindled and ſpotted Sons
of Liberty, that ſhake the Foreſt with their
Roar: now gliding thro' flowery Meads
in copious Streams of perſuaſive Eloquence;
anon a Flame purged from all earthly Droſs
into pure Element. But however undiſtin-
guiſhable at firſt from the Forms it aſſumes,
Firmneſs and Perſerverance will reduce it to
its genuine State, and diſcover the Impoſ-
ture. This, Sir, you have done with Abi

lities

lities which all applaud, and to which even your difappointed Enemies cannot refufe their Teftimony. Thofe Abilities were not before known in their full Extant. You had neither Opportunities, nor a Scene opened to you, in which you could difplay them. Planted in the Shade you pined beneath the Umbrage of an older and unfociable Companion : The Laurel that beggars the Soil on which it grows, ftints every Plant within the Reach of its Influence. Tranfplanted from thence, your Growth has been amazing; and your Roots are fpread wide and deep in the Bofom of your Country. Accuftomed to fee one Man fuperior in the Cabinet, and unrivalled in the Senate, we now fee another incomparably his Superior in that Knowledge, to which now the Preference in both is due. Your Integrity, like his, is free from any venal Stain; and you have both given equal Proofs of clear Hands and fcrupulous Confciences in the Adminiftration of two great moneyed Departments.

The

The Means by which Mr. P—— had often forced himfelf into the Clofet and Councils of his King, in the late Reign, could be reconciled to Lovers of Monarchy, only by the Services which he rendered to his Country in that extorted Confidence : And few can wifh for a Repetition of thofe Means now, with many aggravating Circumftances, but from a Conviction of the fame Neceffity, which clearly does not exift.

In you, Sir, we have a Minifter not obtruded upon his Mafter, confeffedly equal to the high Poft in which you are placed by his free Choice ; and while your Country has a better Chance of being ferved by your Abilities, that Service is not earned at the Expence of a Strain upon regal Authority, which wounds our Conftitution in a vital and effential Part.

The Sufferings of Individuals, however affecting, are a private Concern ; Prejudice

dice alone can make it public: But Violence offered to Majefty interefts the whole.
And furely a young King under that Circumftance, endowed with every Virtue
that commands Veneration, and with every
Quality that wins Love ; gentle in his Difpofitions, munificent in his Nature, loving
his native Country, and demonftrating that
natural Affection, by more and greater Sa-
crifices of private Intereft in three Years,
than recommend the longeft Reigns of his
Royal Predeceffors; offers an Object as
worthy of infpiring the tendereft Emotions,
as they can pretend to be, whofe Picture
I have already endeavoured to draw, even
in the ftrongeft Colours of partial Friendfhip. But fhould fuch a Prince be tra-
duced, reviled, and infulted by unprovoked
and ungrateful Men; fhould their ungene-
rous, unmanly, and brutal Rage, violate
every Regard of Decency and Refpect due
to the Sex and Rank of thofe neareft and
deareft to him ; indignant Refentment
fhould take place of every other Paffion,
and the Abettors of fuch Infamy fhare in

the

the general Execration of its ignominious
Authors. Compaſſion towards ſuch Men
would be criminal Weakneſs. · · The Merits
of the longeſt Life, conſumed in the moſt
diſintereſted Service, would be all cancel-
led by ſuch Baſeneſs, and whatever there
might have been of Rigour in that Treatment of which they before complained, it
would then have been no more than an
Anticipation of Puniſhment, now juſtly due
to their Crimes.

That there are ſuch Men is as certain as
that there are others, fatally linked with
them in the Intereſts of Hope or Revenge,
who abhor their Conduct : the good and
the great Earl of *Hardwicke* died lamenting
thoſe Exceſſes in his Friends, which he in
vain endeavoured to ſtem by his Counſels ;
and in the Spirit of Wiſdom, altho' I hope
not of Prophecy, foretold the ruinous Effects of inebriating Popularity, which threat-
ned the Monarchy he loved, and the Family he had long and faithfully ſerved.
The Bitterneſs of theſe Reflections was,
however,

however, fomewhat foothed in his laft
Hours, by the Part which his Son bore,
in Oppofition to that monftrous Doctrine,
that Parliamentary Privilege fhould be held
facred in the Perfon of him, whofe Abufe
of Parliament tended to prove, there was
no Reverence due to that venal and polluted
Body, for fo it was reprefented by him,
from which alone his Pretence to Privilege
could be derived. The Danger and Ab-
furdity of fuch Tenets, rendered more dangerous by a judicial Determination, alarmed
the Son of our expiring Patriot, who, upon
this Occafion, broke loofe from thofe Connections, which held in Shackles the Minds
of many others; and he fpoke with a
Strength of Argument, a Compafs of Knowledge, and a Clearnefs and Energy of Ex-
preffion, which feemed the Emanations of
his Father's Soul.

Many there are, who from various Motives and Incidents had contracted Connections, which infenfibly drew them into
lengths much farther than they ever pro-
pofed

pofed to go, or ever thought would become neceſſary.

Many, in the Sallies of Mirth, and the Warmth of Wine at thoſe feſtal Boards, where the formidable *Cotterie* was firſt planned and modelled, had entered into haſty Engagements, which cooler Thought and better informed Reflection ſoon condemned. In thoſe Scenes, calculated by the Deſigning to captivate the Unwary, where nothing ſerious ſeems to be admitted, Declarations are made, Opinions are delivered, Libations are poured out to the God of the Feaſt ; and the wild Effuſions of Jollity are afterwards conſidered as ſolemn Vows plighted at the Foot of an Altar.

Such are the Arts by which many have been gained. Spirited Youth loves Oppoſition ; for Oppoſition has the Air of Liberty. It is Exerciſe to the Mind, recommended by its Violence ; the Vehemence of the Chace, well adapted to the Eagerneſs of the Purſuers, who delight in con-

G   tending

tending with Difficulties, and over-leaping
Bounds. Vanity (and Youth is ever vain)
had the Applaufe for which it panted.
Every Inftance of Zeal was fure of this
Reward, and the Hollowers and Feafters
of the Party had their Share of that Praife,
which was profufely poured upon thofe
who difplayed their Talents in florid Ora-
tory. Another and more fubftantial Reward was in view, and feemed at one time
within their Reach, in a Divifion upon a
Queftion well attended and long and
warmly debated. Then it was that lively
Imagination, fanguine Hope, and Prefump-
tuous Ambition fprung into the Lobby,
fure of Succefs, with a Vehemence and Im-
petuofity of Gefture and of Voice, ill fitted
to the Place ; and their tumultuous Num-
bers were nearly equal to their Expecta-
tions of Victory; for the Queftion was car-
ried againft them by ten only.

Such was the State of Oppofition, when
you opened a Scene, exciting other Paffion, and demanding other Cares. You
expofed

expofed, in Facts that could not be falfified, and in Figures that cannot lye, the Ruin impending over a Nation, difpeopled by its Victories, and exhaufted by its Conquefts. The triumphant Author of this Calamity was pointed out, without being named, by the Exceffes which marked the Refplendent Æra of his Adminiftration. His Friends were filent, for the Charge was unanfwerable; or if it could be anfwered, their Abilities were not Abilities of Bufinefs. A Fit of Illnefs faved him from the mortifying Neceffity of being one of that dumb Audience, or of being difgraced in an unequal Combat between Affertion and Facts, Painting and Reality, Declamation and Argument.

The Lovers of their Country fhudered at her Situation ; the Interefted feared for themfelves ; the Thoughtlefs reflected and were convinced. Thefe looked up to you for their Deliverance, while petulant Oppofition hung her Head and departed. Thus in a few Hours of one Day, the Induftry

duftry of many Months was defeated, a dead Calm immediately fucceeded to the Turbulence of an agitated Multitude ; and you, who tottered to your Fall, now ftand firm and immoveable in the Opinion of your Friends, and the Conviction of many reconciled Adverfaries.

F I N I S.